A PRISMA⊤

Also by Grevel Lindop
from Carcanet

Tourists

GREVEL LINDOP

A Prismatic Toy

CARCANET

Acknowledgements

Grateful acknowledgement is due to the editors of the following periodicals, where some of these poems have appeared:
The Light of Peace (Wat Dhammakaya, Bangkok); Numbers; Poetry Book Society New Poems 1988; Poetry Book Society New Poems 1990; Poetry Durham; PN Review; Samatha Newsletter; Siren; Strawberry Fare; Temenos.

'Clun Castle', 'Jets' and 'Intersection' appeared in a pamphlet, *Moon's Pallet*, published by Words Press of Child Okeford, Dorset, in 1988.

First published in 1991 by
Carcanet Press Limited
208-212 Corn Exchange Buildings
Manchester M4 3BQ

British Library Cataloguing in Publication Data
Lindop, Grevel *1948-*
A prismatic toy.
I. Title
821. 914

ISBN 0 85635 921 1

The publisher acknowledges financial assistance
from the Arts Council of Great Britain

Set in 10½pt Imprint by Bryan Williamson, Darwen, Lancashire
Printed and bound in England by SRP Ltd, Exeter

For Esmond and Jackie

The eye…has thoughts of its own, and to see is only a language!
— Coleridge

Dans une rue, au coeur d'une ville de rêve,
Ce sera comme quand on a déjà veçu:
Un instant à la fois très vague et très aigu…
— Verlaine

Contents

III

I

Games of Chance

One summer my grandfather broke his toe
tripping on the steps outside his bank
(this must have been in 1910 or so).
For weeks he sat at home to read and think

and contemplate, his bandaged foot propped up,
the view that spilled down from his third-floor window.
Some thoughtful friend lent him a telescope:
there was the whole of Liverpool below –

cranes, shipping, church spires poking from the ribbed
ploughland of terrace-housing; and just level
with his chair, sandstone-buttressed, scaffold-webbed,
the rising ramparts of the new cathedral

tended by busy ants. Turn the brass ring,
ease in the tube: pink stonework streams and floats,
the limpid circle catches two men perching
high on a half-built pinnacle, playing cards.

The game went on all afternoon. Next day
it was the same: up scaffold, play till noon,
hoist a few blocks, move some planks this or that way,
smoke, look at the paper, and play on.

What would you do? Grandfather thought he'd take
a hand, and wrote a letter to the foreman.
The games stopped. Did the players get the sack?
The story loses focus from there on.

'They never fathomed,' I remember hearing,
'how anyone could possibly have known...'
And how could we know that? There's always something
tempts us to push a story to conclusion

beyond the facts. Grandfather won the trick
anyhow. Was it an unfair move?
Perhaps, perhaps. I can only sit back
balancing issues too fine to resolve

at this distance, except through composition,
the skilled thumb fanning out the knaves and queens,
the bankhand's flourish. I pick up my pen.
Seventy years: a long time between turns;

but I have played the wild card, poetry,
that reliable trump I took good care to hoard
until the right moment. Now, please, may we agree
that the game is over, that I sweep the board?

To Catrin, at Dawn

I wake at six to give you Ventolin
from the Oral Dispenser
shaped like a hypodermic without the needle.
You suck it like a teat,
gulping the sweet
syrup, greedily indifferent
to salbutamol, as to the asthma
that's had you down six times so far this year.

Just one year old,
you've spent more nights in hospitals than I.
Now you're ready to play:
I leave you toys, a drink, two quilts
inside your small stockade
and tiptoe on the stairs
as if a misplaced foot might crack
your bright unblemished dawn,
the clear smooth breathing you've achieved again.

Our curtains still exclude the blinding sun.
I sink my cheek into the cold
imagined alp
of a pillow, skiing the weightless drift
towards sleep. Irresponsible
at last: no need to watch your stomach
balloon, collapse, labouring to catch
thick granular breath...In my dream
you grow into a multi-coloured flower,

some prismatic toy
smiling and refracting light
effortlessly. May you attract kindness
that way, and give it back,
and may that be your beauty, as it is.
Stumbling partly
awake, I start to think maybe
my life has been too complicated.
May you find ways of breathing easily.

Pansies

i

Grouped for the school photograph
they're uncannily alike:
nodding and denying and resuming
their windblown interested poise, each neck a craned green spring
to pinch the bow of its inksoaked silks,
indelible violet saturating the primrose-
rinsed cleanliness of its bib,
Pekinese waffle of pollen and an arched
minuscule tongue-tip lurking in deprecation,
as if at a touch of the pen the inkstain spreading
along each petal, growing
a Rorschach blot-butterfly, Psyche's purples, the way in.

ii

Open the box, turn the mirror over:
and there is such a blush of shadows,
the tigering enigma is a whole unspeakable
opening of flat dark pathways
into energies sudden and slow at the back
of being, of the mind, these are splashes
from an unquestioned pool
asleep, deeper than self, dreaming itself
into raptures and material patterned
blisses that foil and mantle
at the surface of light
drinking, drinking us as we drink them.

iii

Thoughtflowers, nightflowers,
Jacobean masquerade
crowding the hedgerow of my untidy garden,
heartshaped escutcheon and winestained hatchment,
ruffled shadowpinks, glimpses of love surprised,
flaring like headlamp dazzle
against dark velvet,
filmy and resilient in the cold winds of April,
hedge-courtiers teasing
with the flutter of their old names:
love-in-idleness, live-in-idleness,
kiss-me-at-the-garden-gate,
three-faces-under-a-hood,
cull-me-to-you.

1985: Dreaming the Comet

A sill of worn green-painted wood,
A window open before dawn:
Barefoot in the mild air I stood
To watch above the starred horizon

A swallowtail of dusty gold
Stream upward from the comet's eye,
While in an unfamiliar, tumbled
Bed in the room behind, you lay

Until I called you and you came
And by the window took my hand.
What powers calibrate the dark
Reflector of the dreaming mind?

What fine adjustment brought us there
And let me call you from your sleep
Into my dream, to seem to share
That distant, enigmatic shape?

Winchester Cathedral

Eyes do not notice
the hand's acknowledgement,
burnish of caressed oak
or whose face you touch
as you step down from the choir stalls.

You walk between his two masks:
brow moulded back into leaves,
eyelet-holes between the fronds,
foliate lip and beard –
a savage concentration

stares out of the wood
towards the high altar.
Barely noticed
between choir and nave
he guards our comings and goings –

a part of the mystery.
Did man fall and rise by a tree?
Over all our world
the forests are burning.
This church is founded on brushwood.

Househusband

The baby sleeps soundlessly
overhead: she has emptied her
brief charge of irritable
hope and frustration in their medium
of scratchy tiredness, poured them
out in a small flood of crying
and now I can feel
a silent contented purring
lull down through the ceiling;
wind flutters the classical
chorusline of nappies,
their austere flutings
tinged white-gold
with the dry April light. No-one
needs food yet. The fridge
hiccups and sings
in its sleep. At the end of the garden
the bare oak and budding
lilac propose their structures
against a sky white as
paper, translucent as time.

Hide and Seek

Udder-deep in buttercups the cows
swayed past and we stopped to admire them,
the swinging dewlaps, profound child-friendly eyes,
glistening jaws with their somnolent rhythm;

then climbed a bank littered with dogrose petals
and found the burnt-out hulk of a Ford Cortina,
a tarblack skeleton of blistered metals
in a circle of scorched grass. Venturing nearer

(paternal, protective), I peered in. Rusty springs,
some clotted wiring, paper-ash. I turned
to tell you it was safe. You weren't there. Things
lurched slightly. Suddenly there was a flat sunpatterned

surface in every direction: layers of leaf,
pieces of sky and path, that car. I called you.
Silence. Again? Silence, and no relief
in the fidgety mesh of woodland that concealed you

like a puzzle-picture. Somewhere in this drawing
a four-year-old girl is hidden. Can you find her?
Thickets, deep meadows, gravel-pits. Walking, calling,
I could see helicopters, police dragging the river.

There was a flavour I recognized. It was the taste
of nothing. Once in Turkey crossing the Sea
of Marmara the ferry slowed, reversed
and began a laborious circling. Someone told me

a child had fallen overboard, no-one knew
quite how or when. We all hung over the side
scrutinizing a placid unbroken swell, the blue
idyll that had unbelievably swallowed

someone's life. That flavour was in the air
then: a blankness, an unappeasable nothing.
I tasted it again, scanning slopes of briar,
shouting, wandering back to the first clearing

where you stepped out from an elder-clump, very pleased:
'I was playing hide and seek!' What could I do
but toss you into the air and scold you, dazed
as the mind engaged with its happiness and the new

misty sunlight rippled the trees? Meaning
and goodness are natural; only a small part of me
couldn't look away yet from that ferry, churning and churning
its useless circle on an empty sea.

Optics

i Contact Lenses

How many times have you dropped on one knee,
a wounded nymph, one hand
cupped at your eye, your hair blown back,
containing tears against the wind,
then staring into your palm
tensed for a moment and caught
like a crystal tear dabbed up
on a fingertip and considered
silently on the tongue,
that lens? Cleared of grit,
the eye gulps it again
and we forget it, except at night
when everything goes lazy
as the lenses are put to bed;
or when you lose one, jolted
by a baby's flung fist, a sudden false step
or a missed catch when removing it.
From there the stories begin:
the legendary boyfriend who picked one up on a beach;
that last dogged search when, after midnight,
having turned every soft bear end over end and side
over side with the pressureless delicacy
of a computer-graphics program,
I saw it shining, a pool of love and reassurance
in the desert of fluff and crumbs on the floor of the toybox;
and one we never found, that dropped
on an empty country road we scrutinized
until the quartz and granite chippings and the nubbly tar
between them seemed to pave
my retina but yielded
no blessed gleam until we walked away, leaving cars
or sheep to pulverize the lens as I suppose it lies
today, scattered like the fragments of our
perceptions, where a moment earlier
the humped green and mottled
sheets of mountains had gone weightlessly through,
blowing or silting, a fine crystal dust
under Red Bank and Silver How.

[handwritten marginalia: First time I've seen a reference to this in poetry July 17th 1993]

ii Binoculars from Nevilledale Terrace
For Gareth Reeves

Someone has cut this fuzzed chimney out of a magazine
and glued it slap across the pernickety castle
scissored from yellow newsprint. Shreds of ash
blown from a charred edge, the jackdaws tack and spin
in depths of gusty silence. That house of grey cards
is a slate roof and prodigiously above it blooms
a soft green web of tiny handstitched allotments,
two slant rows of lettuces like french knots
and the misty velour of an unreached emerald lawn, cut
by the hard mesh of a budding tree, fluffball
sparrows preening and dropping into space
just within grasp as it seems though I cannot
find my own hand or give it substance to clutch
for anything in this delusive globe of air.
Just a delusion also the pool, mirror-still
(reflecting dark trees and a small green gazebo),
which under my longing scrutiny reverts
to a triangle of dry grass where someone has stacked
higgledy-piggledy the panels of a dismantled shed.
Waving tentatively, scratching his ear,
peering thoughtfully into a dustbin,
here is a neighbour. As he climbs into his car
it seems each detail is of great significance –
the white smoke flowering from a slender chimney,
a lozenge of grass sprigged with neatly-crossed headstones
standing up in real 3-D in this realm
where secrets are so vulnerable to the weightless observer
skimming with the birds, who feels himself become
the deepest secret of all, as if invisible
through seeing too much, as if set free
by inability to touch a single thing
in the landscape though every heartbeat shakes it lightly.

Let me pick up my father's kaleidoscope,
a triangular tube sealed in vermilion paper,
at one end a small boy's eye and at the other
french windows and a syringa tree, lost
as the left eye closes and the mind accepts
a soft-lit mandala of rainbow fragments

fanned open and floating like a Japanese paper
flower in a bowl of shadow. I could have lost
myself in that box of mirrors, adoring the fragments
of light poised by an order that accepts
each jolt, jar, shake as pretext for another
symmetrical unfolding; but the kaleidoscope

gets heavy, trembles, I must drop it – the fragments
of memory live in the body – I feel the kaleidoscope
pried from my fingers; the skin round my eye accepts
an odd cold pressure, its after-image. Like paper
cut-outs, green, violet, orange, ghosts of the lost
retinal rose-window drift from one wall to another

and purple themselves into blotchy darkness, lost
as I duck into sunlight by the french windows. Other
patterns unfurl and complicate: a kaleidoscope
of pink phlox, grass-clippings, wallflowers, leaf-framed fragments
of forgotten garden-corners, the pearly-paper
shiver of honesty by the hedge. One accepts

that imagination orders memory, accepts
that the mind's mirrors multiply sevenfold all the fragments
experience brings them. But in the honesty's paper
trembling I catch reflected a glimpse of the other
I was then, in a world lucent as a kaleidoscope,
richer in its permutation of known things. Lost

and happy I nuzzle the glass and wait for another
revelation. And here is my mother, whose hand accepts
my small grip while she opens the windows. A lost
sweet garden-wind surges, one swinging pane makes a kaleidoscope
where the mock-orange heaves and explodes in symmetrical fragments,
snowing until the steps are as white as paper.

No limit to the diffusion of the fragments,
the prisms of words that will break down the white of the paper;
the ghost-spectrum of mother-of-pearl, grasped-at and lost.

iv The Magnifying Glass
with the Compact *Oxford English Dictionary*

Dipped into the troughs of print
like a wire ring into bubble-mixture,
the black handle floats up
a segment of page bellied out
to the gentle camber of the lens,
serifs of headwords leaking
rainbows of chromatic aberration.

Words, those breath-bubbles:
their meniscus stretching, stretching to encompass
so little! As you bring up the lens
there is a point beyond definition
where the words start to blur and twin,
the parallax of different eyes can't be resolved,
the right word doesn't exist.

Sometimes, tired of searching,
you might give up, spend hours browsing through
supplement, corrigenda, spurious words, books quoted –
or stow the too-heavy volumes away
and lift the lens to the window,
prop up your page and idle the glass to and fro
to catch the filmy, inverted

miniature slide of rooftop and floating cloud
the light spills meticulously
into your room. Serendipity
and the perspectives of idleness
have their place. That summer afternoon,
say, of the partial eclipse: warned
by neighbours squinting through old negatives

and the three-year-old in the alley
with her father's welding-mask –
a slotfaced helmet on two whitesocked legs –
you turned from the sun and focused it to a neat
bitten disc the size of a shirt button,
a fiery tadpole, a light comma that smoked
and burned itself into the paper.

The Project for a New Linguistics

It will listen to the voice of the rose crying, to
    the stone's solitary vowel.

It will be founded in the experience of the diligent
    girl from whose lips fell pearls and rubies; of
    her lazy sister who found herself uttering adders
    and toads.

It will attend to the Tibetan sacred books whose syllables
    murmur themselves perpetually as they rest on the
    shelves wrapped in their rainbow silks.

It will have time for the child's first pun; for the
    old man's explanation of his life.

It will trace the calligraphy of swifts and note the
    pitches of their call.

It will eat the white snake.

First and last it will know one thing, that poetry is
    plain speaking.

The Day

1

The dark's gone. I don't want to go to bed
any more. I think it's breakfast time,
the window's pink. Are you awake, Gerard?
He breathes a noise like water. I won't climb on him.

This other room curtain keeps in the darkness.
The folded bits in the corner look out like monsters
so I flap the daylight open and turn them into clothes.
The dark hair shiny on the cushion's Mummy's,

all this side's Daddy's bed and he's asleep
like a mountain under the coloured squares
except where his beard comes out and his face turns up.
He'll look at me if I can open his eyes.

2

I want the blue dress. I can do it myself.
I'm lost in the scratchy blue, my face is getting stuck
finding the hole. When I pull far enough
the light breaks open and it's round my neck.

Don't do my ears. The noise gets squeezed out of them
then comes back wet. The flannel's cold and hot,
sore on my skin. The white towel bundles like a snowstorm.
When it catches me I'll push my face into the soft.

3

We're at the seaside. This is a boat. You climb
up the ladder on to the top bunk bed
and jump into the duvet. Then you can swim.
Gerard sat down on me and banged his head

because I couldn't breathe. But he's all right.
I won't say anything. I'm a good girl really.
He mustn't pull my hair. O he's pulling it *out*,
O he hurt me and he's a naughty boy.

I push my feet into the holes of the banister
because nobody at all's got to see me.
Then I swing round the corner to look in the mirror,
to see what my face was like when I did cry.

4

You can suck the pear or bite it. Now
it's a moon, now it's a boat, now it's a camel.
The black ones are pips or ladybirds. I bite it so
I don't eat them. Now it's a man on a bicycle.

I'll make this into a building on the table.
Gerard's coming. He mustn't knock it down
but he can make his spoon go through the tunnel
if he likes. I think he can't reach. He's a boy clown

and I'm a girl clown. I get off the chair carefully
to dance with him. This is my hat. O it keeps falling
on the floor. This is the circus and I'm doing ballet,
my head-over-heels. I'm a snow-kitten dancing.

5

The tree's hair's full of acorns. We made a pie
with acorns and earth, and put it in the oven.
Then we got all the leaves and made pastry
with rough edges. We'll take it out when it's done.

I picked a bunch of flowers called chives. If you walk
on the green it smells strong. Over the tree was a plane
writing lines on the sky like a piece of chalk.
We found a moon but then we had to come in

and there was another moon out of the window.
She's got a face. She comes out when the sun
goes round the other side. We're having tea now.
The milkbottle top on the table looks like a moon.

6

We had a story. Mr Punch went shopping
with Baby Marmaduke and the crocodile,
to the supermarket. Judy told them to bring
baked beans and sausages. Marmaduke's a girl,

and she wanted any money to buy a gingerman.
The crocodile knocked over all the tins,
the lady's dog chased him and Mr Punch got bitten.
They forgot to buy anything except the beans.

Mr Punch lives in our yellow house.
When he came home Judy hit him, so he was sorry.
Marmaduke climbed up and ate all the sausages,
then they went to bed and Judy told them a story.

7

Is it dark in the garden? I want lots of books.
I'll go to sleep but I won't close my eyes.
I think this book's a bit frightened because of the fox.
I'll have the soldier, Cinderella and the Three Bears.

Now I'll dream that I'm just in my bed reading.
The water runs in the cupboard. I can hear the owls
and see the long triangle of light floating
over the shoe-house hidden in the hills.

You can come with me if you like. It's slowly
because the door's quite small. But they won't shut it,
the crocodile's kind. Look, he gives me an ice lolly.
He sees my finger but he doesn't bite it.

Initials
Versions of three poems from Rilke's Book of Hours

i

Da neigt sich die Stunde und ruhrt mich an...

The hour falls, touches me; its stroke
metallic, clear, shaking the mind
to resonance. I feel: I can: I take
hold of the day to mould it in my hand.

Until I saw it, nothing was complete;
all was unrealized, poised in its becoming.
Now every glance is consummate: to each
comes, like a bride, the one desired thing.

Nothing is too small for me. Loving
without reservation, I lift up, magnify,
paint each thing on its gold ground; not knowing
whose soul, or by which detail, is set free.

ii

Ich liebe meines Wesens Dunkelstunden...

I am in love with the dark hours of my being,
depths where thought can steep itself and find,
as in old letters, my daily life already
lived-out, distant and subdued as legend.

Out of them comes the knowledge that I have
room for a second life, timeless, spacious;
and sometimes I am like the tree
ripe and murmuring above a grave,
fulfilling the dream which the forgotten boy,
bound and cradled snug in the roots' embrace,
lost in his songs and his unhappiness.

iii

Ich lebe mein Leben in wachsenden Ringen...

I live my life in widening circles
that reach to encompass things; though I
do not know if the last can be completed,
yet I must try.

I circle round God, round that ancient tower,
and have circled millennia long
and still do not know if I am a falcon, a storm
or a great song.

Patchwork

I

Rooms in a house, leaves from a calendar:
The season-coloured squares, humped or askew
As sleep disposes or desire may stir
The wedding-present quilt that covers you,
Hint at some pattern that might just embrace
Both of us. Now I join you in the gulf
Of dark and warmth, of half-sleep and its scarce
Pictured insights, dream-coded, even self
(My love) dissolves; and what I find's a weave
Where thought, love, time, sense, lack come to the same
Rich text. Patchwork, dreamwork, can we achieve
What's promised by the heart's perpetual game –
The intricacies of the work as planned,
Pieced from whatever fragments come to hand?

II

Pieced from whatever fragments come to hand –
A bird-sown rowan clutching at the sky,
Lilac, rough grass, the new fruit trees we try
Lagging against the cold so that they stand
In straw and polythene – our garden's grand
Plan hasn't yet cohered. This year we'll try
Harder. A primrose's pale, lucid eye
Opens to February wind, where panned
Rainbeaten earth begs for some digging. Spring
Should help. Even child-punished grass revives;
Pansies, sweetpeas and random feverfew
Will scrawl their patterns in, recovering
Flowerbeds, flagstones, turf slabs drifted with leaves,
The season-coloured squares humped or askew.

III

The season-coloured squares humped or askew,
Pasture and cornfield tilt against the cloud,
Oak copse and spruce plantation standing proud
To hem a sky of slate- or china-blue;
A short steep lawn, and swallows dipping through
A gulley where the shallow stream is loud
With children's voices, shrilling as they crowd
Barefoot in stony pools... Echoes renew
Far off on this cool urban day: a dream,
Those happy fragments of last summer seem –
Eyed peacock butterflies shivering flowers
Of a baroque nasturtium; pigeons that purr,
Musical through a warmth of lazy hours,
As sleep disposes or desire may stir.

IV

As sleep disposes or desire may stir
You close yourself into a single curve
Or stretch – a webbed heraldic spread of paw,
Translucent hooks quivering in milkwhite fur.
Your delicate and monumental nerve
Makes you at home: white pepper demascened
With ink-black, you fulfil some secret law
Of art and hospitality. We prefer
A house with a cat. Your small liberties serve
To keep surprise awake: velvet jigsaw-
Piece that fits anywhere, you've contravened
The patchwork's grid; now you burrow from view,
Just twitching, with one paw that's nicely preened,
The wedding-present quilt that covers you.

V

The wedding-present quilt that covers you
Is Hotch-potch, technically: no formula
Dictates its colour-patterning; a far
Subtler rhythm and counterpoint leads into
An art that hides itself, pleased to eschew
Cathedral Window, Clamshell, Compass Star
For the harmonics of the half-familiar,
The sprigged clashed cottons fading and made new.
Luxuriance cropped, leafscroll and flower entwine
Across the field bordering a white-flecked square
Of blue; splashed colours run but know their place
Like hopscotch; matched, apart, almost a pair,
Harlequin check and tendrilled columbine
Hint at some pattern that might just embrace.

VI

Hint at some pattern that might just embrace
The darkening fragments of a day, the dull
Ache that's a residue of hours too full
Of half-done jobs, an urge to plunge the face
Into cool water or sheer emptiness
Unreached by children's cries? I can't, the spell
Of love dissolved in sleep's too strong, the lull
Where all thought's poised. Your arms make me a space
That's timeless, non-Euclidean, maybe known
Only to lovers speechless and alone
Together. Harmonies of breath dissolve
Our rigid forms; a gentle chaos plays
Linked hearts' impulsive rhythms, softly frees
Both of us, now I join you in the gulf.

VII

Both of us, now I join you in the gulf
Between worlds, daughter, claw sleep's cobweb-film
From different sides. I rock, to break your rhythm
Of gulped breath and loud heart; you shine the width
Of dream-glazed pupils on me, a vexed sylph
Hunted through forest mazes. All this month
The moon's tugged at our dreams, August's shut warmth
Conjuring fretful goblins horsed on wasp
Or blundering beetle out of the hair's-breadth
Tideshifts of sleep; wild garlic, cuckoo-pint
And honeysuckle sweetening the faint bilge-
Tang of the summer ditches. Let the dream-wolf
Unclench. Love's a cool spring to wash the depth
Of dark and warmth, of half-sleep; and it's scarce.

VIII

Of dark and warmth, of half-sleep and its scarce-
Acknowledged glimpses of sleep's threshold, tracks
Spilt and diverging in their own strange light
Embossed with niggly visions, here's a place
Perhaps to speak. Who we are waking lacks
The knowledge of its sleeping partner, drawn
On the breath's thread into the maze of night
Whose cryptic loot the morning memory bears –
A music-book, a staircase, a blue tax-
Return unfilled. And somewhere, out of sight,
Bathed in dark waters, bringing when reborn
Confused, oracular, to its daylight half
What gifts through gates of ivory or horn?
Pictured insights, dream-coded; even self.

IX

Pictured insights, dream-coded, even self-
Mirrored and rippling fantasies give way
To sun, birdsong, the magpies' raucous fray
Among the oakleaves and, waking the half-
Light by the door, a boy, who hauls himself
On to our sill to watch the sparrows play
Along the roof. The images of day
Are odder than the night's and ask more love,
You face the labyrinth with not one thread
But a whole tangle. My son climbs up to me,
Nestles into my shoulder. But sleepyhead,
We're late. Enmeshed, I hurry, snap, get angry.
Forcing the day like a wrong-side-out sleeve,
My love dissolves, and what I find's a weave.

X

My love dissolves, and what I find's a weave,
Jacquard of themes repressed one moment, up
And forcing others down the next, to leave
Only confusion and remorse; on top
No pattern, just the ends from a sheared crop
Of misplaced wants. How to love people seems
Harder than how to please oneself; to cope
With them's far messier than writing books
Or being simply alone. They get their hooks
Well into you, and tear. Then you recall
They're you, there is no solitude, writing looks
Out from their height. Without them what it all
Comes to is nothing, and poetry's a game
Where thought, love, time, sense, lack come to the same.

XI

Where thought, love, time, sense, lack come to the same
Realm of clear possibility yet lose
No bulk, edge, colour, force, the word we use
Is art. Kindled in solitude, a flame
Draws to its current clarity of aim
The whole vortex of mess, breaking to blues
That line a linen sky or interfuse
Shadows under the rose mountains to frame
A moment poised in an embroidered field
Where we stood once. Your thread sows through the sheaf
Of Ceres' hair knots of silk poppies, sealed
Right by their own random proportion. Weave
On weave, pen, needle, heart, what unrevealed
Rich text, patchwork, dreamwork can we achieve?

XII

Rich text, patchwork, dreamwork, can we achieve
An oracle that tells us what we want
To know, truths no-one asks us to believe,
Numinous trusts whose fragile margins haunt

Thought and decision? The one who made this quilt
For our marriage-bed later walked out
From her own husband and her children, spilt
Something she must have gathered, and no doubt

Read in herself whatever made her leave.
The gift stays on, and so far I've divined
No want in it, except maybe to give
Others a happiness she couldn't find.

Perhaps we want the things we want too much,
Dragged by a look, a memory, a name...
Imagining we'll be allowed to clutch
What's promised by the heart's perpetual game.

XIII

What's promised by the heart's perpetual game?
Hunger, addiction, fear, emptiness, blame.
Completeness lies with others, or the dead:
And if they seem the happier, it's because
Their otherness leaves nothing to be said
About their discontent, which is (or was)
The same as ours. A land of lost content
Is radiant in this room, blocked by your long
Fanatical attention to the absent
Abstract and famishing better. Neither wrong
Nor right, the moment offers its unnoticed
Completeness in a breath, a stone, a hand,
While thought builds mazes round your having missed
The intricacies of the work as planned.

XIV

The intricacies of the work as planned
Allured the mind into a maze of dreams –
Lost mirror-gardens, time in fugue with art,
Love laced with language spiralling to reach
Harmonics such as moved the angelic forms
(Breathless, lamplit) to enunciate their laws,
Gracious at Duino and Thoor Ballylee:
Music for magic casements! But the sea
Recoils from those rockfast and rumoured shores,
The tide of words is racked with tedious storms,
Turbid with residues. We comb the beach,
Turn up each word and try it on the heart;
Offer the gods our harsh, tentative themes,
Pieced from whatever fragments come to hand.

XV

Pieced from whatever fragments come to hand –
As a called ghost might improvise a face
From crumpled linen, or as you might trace
The bow's note patterned out in dancing sand –
Ideas take form, rhythms and years evolve
Subjective pastorals, where we cultivate
Our rooms, our hearts, our words to celebrate
Small feasts or hurts, and harvest a resolve
To stay, or change. Autumn arrives again,
The days grow short, the lines are running out,
But nothing ends. The year will turn about
With stars or fog, while we try to sustain
Our love, our growth through selves which merely are
Rooms in a house, leaves from a calendar.

For Eric Ravilious

The watercolour glazes of lichen on a garden hose
worming among geraniums might be one
of your monuments; the chalk hill-figure
that pivots on the vantage-point
of a railway-carriage window, another. Failing to return
after an air-sea rescue
off Iceland, you were presumed
lost sketching among the waves; your disappearance
could not have made less noise. Those glassy planes,
those camouflage artists,
paid little or no attention. Still you are not
dead at all. On the contrary
you have become the guardian angel
your work created, keeping
an England of pastels and plain words,
market gardens, china mugs and the peeling
wallpaper in farmhouse bedrooms. Turning
to what we like, your art
accompanies us, a slanting mirror
by which we organize our unambitious loves.

An Edale Sketchbook

January

Fallow under a quarter-moon
Vacant ploughland lets the season
Do as it likes this mild dead day.
Thin wind rakes across the clay
Muddy and pooled at the fields' edges,
Shivers the tarnished-iron thorn hedges
And fades among the papery grass
Still fluttering in wornout pastures.
  Only the sky tumbles with life:
Masses of cloud capricious move
Against the hills' dark parapets,
By turns corrode the silhouettes,
Cubes of black rock at Nether Tor
Melting to tousled rags of air,
And like a wet inkstain Cold Side
Runs at the sky's edge, lost and conjured.
Birds stay low. A kestrel hovers,
Madly flapping, slides across,
Hovers and flaps again, to scan
For movement in the powdered green
Of a sown field below him. Nothing
Takes his eye. The mesh of sowing
Displays its pale maze to the sky.
Catching the wind, he falls away.
  Preoccupied with nearer things,
Trailing the white lace of his wings,
A magpie floats with carrion grace
Stump to stump over the grass,
Content to strut and scavenge here
Among the leavings of a year.
Scavenger too, I cross the field
For what its sheltered corners yield
And find an emblem of the time
Dropped like a discarded costume:
Black wool mask with empty eyes,
A spine distributed like dice,
Gobbets of fleece strewn on the mud;

A thing acceptably dismantled.
The living sheep not far away
Rip the thin grass equably,
Pace between battered henhouses,
Ignore the hens' dishevelled fuss.

   Shoving against my face, the wind
Opens its brief book of sound:
Brawling echo of farmdogs;
Comment of rooks that twirl like flags
Around the rattling treetops; thin
Whine of gears climbing the incline
Up to Mam Nick where the road threads
The hills' rampart between the clouds.

   O January, twofaced god,
Stern guardian of the opening word,
Blank eye and empty mask between
The plangencies of line and line,
Tolerate our endeavour, take
The first note for the finished task,
The first stone for the drystone wall
Articulate along the fell,
The gathered crop for the first seed
Drilled to the slabby, polished clod
Skewed where our ploughing has defined
A threshold to the harrowed ground.
Nourish us with your emptiness,
Your generosities of space,
After the death, before the birth,
The fire shrunk to the clotted hearth.

   Tinge of coalsmoke hugs the village.
Under the porch at Grindsbrook Lodge
The tabby's mask of sepia flame
Broods on the savage rites of home,
Complacently displays the kill,
A dead mouse on the stone doorsill.
I pause: the yellow eyes keep watch.
But I shall not disturb the latch
Or go beyond my boundaries.
Withdrawn, implicit, meaning lies
At rest within particular
Arrangements of mist, stone and fur,
While noon prolongs a muddy calm

As if no other hour would come
With rain to wash away that high
Chalk thumbprint on the marbled sky
Or snow to load those blue milk-crates
Stacked lopsided at the farm gates.

August

Rainbow and millstone grit,
thunder piling into the clouds –
the incongruities of August: shaken ruff
of a black and white sheepdog panting
at the first-floor lintel
of a stone outhouse; spattered rowan
capital illuminating
thickets of green text;
pale stitchery of ashkeys,
deep lanes bedded down in honeysuckle
nettles and purple vetch.
A bridleway like a drystone wall
sunk on its side
in the ground: you walk
on the edges of the slabs
to Grindsbrook, where the Edale shales
hang above the stream
a cliff-face of brittle
leaves, charred edges
of a burnt book, tamped into drift
of flakes, chips, tending down
to grit and sand and the water
sliding over red rock.
    Wind shivers the meniscus
of light: away in the tumbling
haycart of sky the billows
coalesce and the spattering starts
on your hands, blotting the rock,
staining its soft marbled endpapers of lichen;
plucking the stream to gooseflesh, melting the path.
    Underfoot the bleeding of red clay; overhead

raindrift swerves and glitters,
playing fibre-optics where the mists break,
clot, release sheets of sunlight.
August turns her *camera lucida*,
the billion prisms in the raincloud
focusing a stump of rainbow over
Lose Hill. Films of shadow
chase across the fields. The stream
throws itself down the stone in a frigid rococo
of molten glass, air bubbles
racing in wobbling clusters under the fans
and ribs of its fussed vaulting.
   Slower is the flow
of the rocks, their volcanic pour
stilled to a stacking of grainy
black cubes, to piles of soft pennies,
to lion-headed wrinkled
outcrops lipped and dewlapped
with a slabby gruel of lava.
Only the weather pursues this unfinished quarry,
saturating, eroding,
wearing the millstone cheeks
with the unanswerable persistence of water.
Grindsbrook closes in
to a locked cascade of boulders,
water dropping like a secret through fissures,
forgotten unless it emerge a moment
to whirl a handful of quartz pebbles
in the dicecup of a pitted slab.
Palms on the abrasive rock,
you grip to pull yourself
bodily out of the narrow cleft
of the gulley. Light and space
burst with a gust of wind
into your head. And floating
over the long hazed-green drop of the valley,
music: the perpetual, wholly-satisfied,
interminable grumbling lilt of sheep
and a cowman's half-bellow half-yodel:
'*hic – hic – hic – hic – hic – hic …*'
obscure traditional prosody of milking-time.
   Over the streamhead, above you, one more rock,

a massive gritty fungus
or melted anvil cleft in two:
pulling up by the fingertips you gaze
over the top and into a pool
the size of a font: clear water,
your reflection a ragged black
against a translucence of sky
just rippled by wind, poised in a cup of stone.

September

i

The hot sunlight is laid across a slicing cold
of air, so that however warm your skin,
your mind will not be comforted from the longer shadows
even at noon, the overfine gold of the birch leaves,
the too-limpid blue of a summer sky grown fragile,
paler at the edges, the horizons; however hot the rock-
ledge, its hollows are expecting the dew
to pool there and freeze before dawn. Summer's lease
is crumbling; stiffly the rowan proffers
its clusters of scarlet wax, stiffly the unfurled bracken
trembles against an air which will refine it
to its own silhouette, then to its own skeleton,
to gold, to rust, to black and into the earth.

ii

Two squirrels gambol in the intricate
rootcastle of the uptorn beechtree:
iron-red brooch clotted with stones,
fringed with fungal lace of roothair,
galleys and pits for their delight.
No-one observes their shadowplay,
silhouette *obbligato*
cartwheel and arabesque
against the light, into the radical maze.

The river vanishes underground,
no-one hears its nightsong
under the pebbly bed
dry now as a cobbled road,
the high stone wall that dammed it back,
the long iron screw that raised the sluice;
the glassy beads of sound,
ululating echo-vowels,
music warbling in a concrete throat.

iii

When a wall dies its secrets come to light.
A drystone wall lies down like a failed animal,
spilling its entrails out on the grass:
and here is the clean gritstone and limestone,
each cob black on one side like a burnt loaf.
Scratch it and under your nail
are Manchester, Huddersfield, Sheffield,
two centuries of mills
pocked and scored into the Pennines.
Why should anyone cherish that?
Walls grow clean again,
sun bleaches, frost and rain scour;
still nothing sneaks in as once the black winds did.
People die or move on, the trees
carry no black growthrings.
Only the walls remember, netting the valley
from end to end in their hidden veinwork of soot,
their dark secret as long as a wall is a wall.

iv

A girl in a loose coat, a long switch in her hand,
directing with a high call and a gesture of the stick,
training a pair of dogs: they weave across the field
like shuttles trawling invisible thread to cut out one sheep
and pen the others in a corner. Again the high call:
the dogs bound back, the sheep pour out over the field
in a scatter and run like spilt mercury together into one.

v

A mug of tea and a heaped sugar-bowl,
a chair beside the rusting Chrysler in the farmyard.
Green trodden mud; a radio in the kitchen.
From the dairy, the hum of the separator.

vi

Look at the hook on this gate:
smooth as a spoon, it lies in your hand
a heavy iron fish, gill-threaded
by frayed red nylon bailer-twine, its barbed
tongue blunt from latching into the leaf-thin
scrolled iron eye of the gatepost; and, before that,
into other eyes: for the hook is the older.

Since it left the forge
perhaps not a day has passed but some hand
has fed it with hooking, unhooking,
weighing or absently fingering,
tieing or chaining perhaps
once in ten years or twenty to a new post
or a new gate, till its patina
comes to your hand like a greeting
out of the old, imperceptibly
changing world of the metals
that tolerate the abrupt, brief dream of man
crossing a field, closing a gate behind him.

A Playground

It's spring again, and the children are shouting and climbing
on the climbing-frames and demanding to go on the swings
regardless of mud and the wind that shivers their parents.
They are driven to drive, to outshout, to overwhelm things.

And someone thought it was worthwhile spending the money
to give them this place, and someone else spent their time
in design and ingenuity and metalwork
merely so that these could swing and capsize and climb

and amplify in their own way what they are:
living imagination, pure possibility,
what's good in itself. There's hope in that. And moreover,
let them play a little longer, and look, you can see

there a sheer unstillable pool of the water of life:
though countless times polluted, endlessly clear
and renewed from sources immeasurably beyond us,
within us, the permanent spring of the human year.

Language of Flowers

Pink, pansy and leaf
Floated under the lamp
Perfect for that evening;
And what was it they said?
Not your choice or mine,
Going from nowhere to nowhere,
Arriving, always arriving.
This is the answer, they said,
This and again this,
Black penstrokes on the pansy's cheek
As far removed from writing
As eternity from time.
I could think of nothing else
But the flowers. I was utterly ashamed
Of all I could do or be.

Mantra

Everything turns away,
All things arise and fall –
The buzzard turning the hill
Through the jewelled mill of his eye,
The seashell turned to stone
In the slow tides of shale,
The larch lost in cloud,
The shepherd's call on the air.
The pirouetting hare
Patrols the high wood,
Rain polishes rock,
The stone bridge swallows the stream:
Nothing is still the same.
Where is stillness found?
All things arise and turn,
Everything falls away.

Meudon

They talked about great art, and the cafés
Where the new schools of painters spent their days
Drinking, theorizing, purging an inchoate
Slubber of living from the abstract fate
Blossoming onto their canvas stroke by stroke;
Clusters of bells whose echo-ripples broke
The tilting orbit of a flock of doves;
Cold northern light softening in stained alcoves;
Layered silence falling in tall libraries,
Tamped like the leafmould under forest trees;
Walled peace where no excitement could intrude;
Stone harmonies; the gift of solitude.
The Muses lived in Paris, so they said.
    I found a city of the sick and dead,
Tettered with hospitals, scabby with bills
Warning against the pox or offering pills;
Bright droves of wealthy invalids; the gaunt
Genteel shaking with alcohol and want,
The frayed cuffs like the frayed nerves gathered in
As if their clothes grew to a second skin,
Grimed, creased and sickening with the trodden heart;
These houses where the dead are kept apart
From the still living by a single brick,
And you might lie awake to hear the thick
Clenched battle of the phthisic through the wall,
Or muttered conference saddening down the hall.
And worse, perhaps, the eyes: one helpless glance
Seen through the window of an ambulance
Administered a hypodermic shock;
On the Metro, your gaze might meet and lock
With any stranger's, guard it how you try –
I wondered if diseases of the eye
Could spring contagious from some other's thought
Abhorred, glanced-at, succumbed-to, held and caught
For a long moment, until the staggering train
Spilled us into the sightless crowd again.
    That was fatigue: reading so much, the books
Crowded the table, piled like barrel-shooks,
Loose staves to be hooped in one day to hold

New distillations from a childhood world
I was forgetting now I tried to tether
Dreamwork and the tough webs of speech together,
To write, to learn French, to press down some firm
Reading into a mind where thought would squirm
And slide askew in marshy ignorance.
A blind persistence seemed the only chance.
    Sometimes under a hot, green-shaded lamp
I would court dreams rather than face the damp,
Mist-haunted, mud-rinsed pavements I must tread
To climb up to my house's muddled head,
Step off the page, and find myself alone:
Russia, Tibet, a hermitage of stone,
Mountain flowers in summer, winter a dumb
Echoless poem of ice where I could come
To stare into a mirror and not see,
At last, the filthy blemish of the *me*
Masked in its mouldy velvet flesh, constrained
By swathes of self-conceit, meshed-in and stained
With stale desires and grubby fears, a child
Who tried on borrowed costumes and grew wild
With terror seeing his own image pass,
Hawkfaced and alien, in the dusty glass –
Then fall awake to front the choice again,
The cliffs of print, or the flat streets and rain.
    And now, Meudon. An artist and his house,
A solitude of trees grown populous
With thoughts clear as reflections in a blade
Or the bronze faces his own hands have made;
The unpruned roses scattering their flakes
Leafwise in madder, scarlet, crimson lakes;
The peartrees studded with impending fruit;
The waterlily's waxed-paper involute
Where nosing carp disturb the speckled glaze
Or shifting sunlight opens to a blaze
And damsel-flies, unscorched, dither and hold
An instant steady through candescent gold.
How easily the branches hang and hang
Over the walks, sharpening summer's tang
With intimations of a happy fall,
The burdened trees' surrender and renewal,
Exchanging bulk for scope and mass for sky,

A shaped mass for a branching line, while I
Watch Rodin with his arms sticky with clay
Fighting the earth he loves and every day
Coaxing new forms into the reach of sight –
His half-formed figures, blind against the light,
Helped on by stockman's or by midwife's hands,
Brutal or gentle as the work demands.

    I cannot make, or be: the will frustrates
Its own desire; the calm that incubates
Articulate design is warped and split,
The spring fouled by the mouth that thirsts for it.
If I could turn as mindless as those trees
That pattern light through their interstices
Of leaf and twig, evolving hour by hour
Slow fugues of sun, should I wake into power
And find an elemental force transferred,
Crystalline, through the lattice of the word,
Poems sharpveined as leaves dropped on the page?
But mind will not give up its sullen rage
For accomplishment. And so I think and fret,
Walk in the meadows till my shoes are wet,
Come back to dine and hear my host expound
His commerce with those calm gods he has found;
Or write his letters in my limping French,
Dogged apprentice at the master's bench,
Hoping a look, a hand, a word will teach
Some way my baffled selfhood cannot reach.

    Yesterday while we dawdled in the shade
I watched how timidly his daughter played,
Birdlike, near to our feet but not too near,
On the gravel, preoccupied with queer
Patterns of leaves and stones painstakingly
Fetched and laid out in careful symmetry:
Not self-absorbed, absorbed in him, in hope
His glance might just include her in its scope,
Always so broad and steady, so unmoved
By the anxieties of the partly-loved.

    Once she came close and, as he talked, unbent
The fingers of his rough right hand, intent
On fastening in his grip a small bruised flower.
He looked, and looked away, the sleeping power
Of that huge unbraced hand slept on, the mind

Exploring other prospects, not inclined
To alter course because it chanced to strike
So small an object. Is that what God is like,
Or the Buddha? Too perfect to look down
When we give ourselves, or only with the frown
Of perfect absence, like a mirror turned
To throw the sun in our dazed faces, burned
To incognition, seeing nothing, though
The sun might see us and we couldn't know?
    If so, we must become that mirror, make
Ourselves, and all things, God: the poem should take
Our substance from us piece by piece until
We are no-one and nothing, only chill
Transforming fires of art whose touch conceives
Imagined autumns from remembered leaves
Or perfect love from disappointment. Look,
The world exists to end up in a book –
Mallarmé's words. It's time to turn away,
To leave the window for the desk. All day
The garden's swum away into the wind
Beyond the rippled glass. If it has thinned
To a translucent recollection, now
The words may settle into place somehow,
Insects on the meniscus of a stream,
Bright skaters to express a tongueless dream.
        Tugging this desk to face into the wall
I feel a pull that weakens from the small
Innumerable deaths that lure the heart
Back towards human life. To be apart,
Unblemished by the hungers that corrode
Others with what we want of them, to load
Nothing into the balance, to oppose
No purpose to the darkly-shadowed rose
Blooming from death and life, might be the task,
That offering the words themselves would ask.
Sounds express silence, writing empty space
Around the words; before us is a place
Polar, impossible, this whitewashed wall
And empty book through which my hand will crawl
Spoiling the paper, working to reveal
New emptiness for further art to heal.
Our labour is our dwelling-place: no shock

Can harm a house that's founded on a rock
Deep as the abyss that lies under our speech,
Tranquillity no human voice can reach.
I set my course into the snow, alone:
The unmarked page is pure, and hard as stone.

Trojan Voices

'Nos Troia antiqua, si vestras forte per auris
Troiae nomen iit, diversa per aequora vectos...'

Brute, then, taking full view of the island, and searching up the river Thames,
built upon it a City; which, in remembrance of the late subverted Troy, he called
Troynovant, or new Troy, now London. This done, he put his soldiers to tilling
of the earth.

i *Poet*

The battles had all been won or avoided. What could we do
but hone fine blades to a redundant sharpness,
polish our shafts, score points and bullseyes –
the world our butts, firing-range and tiltyard?
Names of the great generals, mighty clogged swordsmen
of old, we recited and praised,
reviewing their strategies on the tabletop –
here a line, there an advance. When we woke up
the war had already started. But not like the old wars: the gods
were nowhere to be seen, both sides were soon
staled, we dug in and stared each other
out over the ditches; year by year soldiers
lounged and joked in pidgin across the checkpoints.
Skirmishes notched the edges of our weapons
but defined nothing except a diseased
persistence. The epic was stillborn. Now
it will be famine, epidemic or a bloody shambles
puts our pride out of its misery
much too late. How wistfully we long
for our previous art, for the connoisseur's approval
of a sword's rhetorical flourish in undivided air!

I would have been a flask of a rare perfume
distilled from spring evenings, the grey corners
of a dusty street where girls whisper together
once, then laugh at a stranger going by;
from the overhearing of parents' talk,
from singing and gossip and a letter,
from hours walking alone by the sea,
dawdling, digging a pebble out of sand
with one toe while the mind bathed
in another depth, inaccessible and protected;
from the unnoticed moments that have no words
to sweep them empty; from the covering quiet as children's voices
        recede,
from the renewal of sunlight when a memory is tasted
for the first time and known at last;
from the exactions of middle-age
which concentrated out of years just one drop of being;
from this empty mirror, these sundried herbs,
silence that turns with the wind all day long.

Drop by drop I would dispense all this
to those who might value its fragrance,
to grandchildren who would not.

Now nothing will be saved.
Let it smash, its essence evaporate,
war tread the shards into the mud;
nothing has the same meaning
as the three-year-old girl who follows
a puff of thistledown
circling
weightless like a sleepwalker
climbing air
in a corner of the yard.
If nothing else goes free let the wind take it,
carry that seed
anywhere out of this time and place.
Let it lodge in a crevice, let it take root and crack stone.

iii *Man*

Where do the Furies come from?
Each of us looks in his heart
and finds the cracks through which they might (or perhaps have
    already)
come. I neglected my father.
I failed to answer that letter.
I thought no-one would notice: I told myself
it was not important, or that it was too big a task
for me, or that she deserved it, or that I
had a right, if there were any justice. Is our trouble now
no justice, or too much?
The Furies, anyhow, are haunting our sleep.
It would be something to meet death complete,
not drag this maimed past of selfishness and botched work.
There is no-one to ask for forgiveness. The forgiveness of the Furies
is that they do not allow us any longer to lie.

iv *Cassandra*

The priests prod the ceremonious offal, thumb their thick books.
I am opened by vision,
split like a tree by lightning, by knowledge
that will not move a feather, though it melts
stone walls and shrivels passers in the street
to walking corpses, carrying their wounds
visible on their breasts or in their hands.
The head is a helmet so easily broken
and the whole face is blind except the eyes
which cannot tell the rest what they see.
People see
and go about their business
while the god's saliva is burning in my mouth,
I cannot spit it out nor can I
swallow and be content, there is nothing for it
but utterance, utterance,
to talk to walls, to stones,
to weeds in the crevices,

to people I can only imagine,
only my enemies because they would believe me.
If the Greek women hear of this, will they understand?
How I waited for the swordsman in Athene's house –
choosing to let it be here, in front of her altar,
reading the future in my own bowels?

v   *Timbers*

Not since the abused dryads
were torn out of the heart of the wood
squealing at axe-blow and plane-rip
have timbers cried out like this
we nurtured our voices
in the whisper of footfall and echo
joistcreak that spoke 'home'
to the preoccupied man
cooling tick of a rafter
spoonclatter banging door
or in luck were cossetted to the surrendered shiver
of a soundboard under a string.

Shamming dead shamming dead
and now a myth has exploded out of our sleep
a blink a quiver a rush we are transformed
to mythological beasts
the pinewall a cataract of light howling upwards
into a turbulence of cloud
the oak rooftree an incandescent mantis
pitched to its knees
groaning into a sea of live tongues
the temple statues the painted
gods with their mouths wide open who had forgotten
they were the hearts of trees remember
where they were going and pour up into a thousand summers'
blinding leafage the roar
of their combined purpose

in the morning our ashes
tangle along the seashore in the wind, drop
and lap in smeared delicate eddies of foam

a black grain silting the ploughed furrows

not caring if they will be ploughed again

vi *Poet*

Burned out with the light of a sum total
amounting at last to zero, I was left
to feel my way with this framework of bones
and a fed skin through the animal world of touch,
knowing collusion of cup with lip, identity
of hand with woven cloth or hair, an ancient kingdom
I had never acknowledged and which seemed
sufficient, the body collaborating,
to follow its own strange laws for ever.

Nothing to do with me either the memories
that spread, clouded and fined above the dry unquestionable
calyx of here and now, a great immaterial spun
seedhead puffing itself as if I were growing
a second mind. Were others like this, was it
a tumour, an infection of being? At last,
to clear my head, I began. I must have cried
but every tear was a word; it was beyond me
or my hearers and I gave in. There seemed
no end to what I knew, but that the knowing
wasn't mine.   Already our language is scattered
like groundsel fluff on the wind, catching at thresholds,
housecorners, unweeded verges. I am singing it
in its own voice and know we are saying goodbye.
If there is a purpose I do not understand it,
or if there are gods or what is poetry.

But the hearers are loud again, they are calling
out of their hunger I can feed but not satisfy
for more than a moment. The back of the skull
opens. I turn with this blind mask
towards them. They want me
to tell them what they have seen.
Until I speak, they cannot believe their eyes.

The Welsh Poppy

Forgotten desires fulfilled
   are the best kind:
her yellow silks uncrumpled
   by the wind

out of their furred green case
   the Welsh poppy now
unplanned, unasked, displays –
   and unrelated to how

some years I scattered seed
   in a different bed,
dug in roots, scrutinized,
   but nothing happened.

Over starry leaves
   green springs unfurl
from weedlike beginnings
   in unpromising soil.

Perhaps there's hope:
   it may be, happiness –
once you have given up
   hope – will come like this.

II

A Month's Dreams

I was reading Proust. For a long time every night
I tried to go to bed early. Often I failed.
But the inner life is not so easily thwarted;
and as Longchenpa wrote, aren't all phenomena
like the shadows cast by a lamp, like the moon in water,
insubstantial, ungrounded, a cloud, a rainbow, a dream?

I found myself interviewing the famous poet
in his sitting-room. He showed me Tom King and Dick Turpin,
Staffordshire murderers, on a ledge over the door.
On his bookcase shone a silver cigar-cutter
shaped like a pike. I asked him if he possessed
a chipping from the Great Pyramid. 'No,' he said,
'but my grandmother does.' When I played back the tape
the loudest sound was the splashing of wine into glasses
punctuated by a small, brisk explosion
each time the poet lit a cigarette.

I gave lunch to a Buddhist monk, and had to drive him
to the station. All the roads were being dug up.
We missed the train and went to sit in the bar
where we were joined by a stranger who wished to ordain.
He questioned the monk, who gave him a tiny Buddha
of gold-coloured metal with indecipherable
script on the back and a small ring at the top
by which it was to be hung on a chain round one's neck.

I was photocopying my dead friend's poems
on a machine in my living friend's study. The intervals
between pages I spent dipping into Francis Barrett's
The Magus, or Celestial Intelligencer –
'the Times, Bonds, Offices and Conjuration of Spirits'.
'A fudge,' said my friend. 'It's supposed to be original,
but most of the contents are stolen from Robert Fludd.'

I went to collect my wife from hospital
and found she was having a baby. The delivery unit
was full, so there she was breathing and groaning
on a bed in the ward downstairs. The Sister predicted
that the child would be born with a caul
and the gift of second sight. In the event
to help the baby along they ruptured the membrane
(possibly also our chances of clairvoyance)
and the birth was normal. It was a boy. I had forgotten
my camera, mirror, sponge, almost everything. The room
glittered round me through a prismatic haze of tears.

A Path

There was a path through the long grass. Although it had rained
we walked dryshod where someone had cut a swathe
over the ground hummocked with graves near the church
to a small gate under the yew, that led out
to pasture where the sheep were settling themselves
in the lee of the drystone walls. Long blades of light
and longer shadows cut across the fields
and we shivered but were happy. Nothing to see,
really, except more small fields and more walls
and the Dale spreading on either side, one green slope
turning a warm gold in the last sunshine and one
already dark as a raincloud, sinking to twilight.
But we were newly married. Everything
was filled with the plenty of its own meaning.
Even the churchyard was changed as we came back:
the long grass by the gate was gone and near the church
was a man with a scythe, just visible in the twilight.
We'd walked out in his first track, and were returning
as he finished the job, the darkening air rich
with the juice of new-cut stalks, the long grass
falling in drifts and the path ahead of us widening
and widening until it was no longer a path.

Dreaming about Oxford

It's a city I must put on like a suit of clothes,
insinuating myself up a college staircase
like an arm snugging into the sleeve of a cashmere sweater.
And though my room isn't here it will be soon,
as soon as dinner's over. Already a throng
in gowns and dinner-jackets is pressing around me:
we're going to chapel, or lunch, and look, there's Bowra
bull-headed and stubby in his grey suit, like a sealion
barking encouragement. 'Ah. Lindop –'
But I'm out of earshot already, and deep in Blackwell's
or is it the Bodleian? Anyhow, here's an alcove
crammed with books, and the alcove is up on a gallery
that's lined with books, overlooking a bookfilled room
with passages opening out of it walled with books.
I begin to leaf through the books. Inside them are gardens,
and in the gardens are buildings and in the buildings
are gardens again with more buildings inside them
(there's no hurry, I can get back to college later,
I've passed the test and know I can stay here forever,
or at any rate for the moment.) I keep going in,
through doors with stone mullions and doors with linenfold panelling
and sluggish unwieldy oaks with lumpy iron nailheads
and panelled deal with white china knobs and gardens
in *trompe l'oeil* perspective painted on seasoned elmboard
and the doors are becoming so many and so close together
I can't tell if I'm opening doors or turning pages.
But things are growing more spacious, the weight on my hands
is only the weight of the sheets, and to open my eyes
admits the morning and the fact that I've woken
for good or ill, though I'm far from certain which.

Curtains

There are two kinds of people, someone said:
the ones who tug the curtains closed at sunset
and those who leave them wide open to night.
If so, and now that I've heard it, I'm one of that sort,
for the summer at least; though a saxe-blue offcut of sky
and a bread-coloured braiding of brickwork are all you can see
from this chair in the afternoon. But over the room
comes, as the shadows spill round, gathering form,
first a haze and then a recession, as if space
withdrew, or relinquished its depth, while the focus
of intensity shifts to somewhere else outside
and the sky starts to astonish you, its shred
of resonant china-blue (crossed by a bird,
a diving jet-black star) yielding to a remote
bell-clear royal blue and an unearthly violet
on which the lamp throws its mirage. Then the abrupt
drop into darkness, glass becoming mirror,
the room restored, a privileged interior
warm-coloured world part of me would reject
when I reach for the curtain and rather pause to inspect
my face, lightpatched, angular, shadow-eyed,
transparent to the unclaimed depth of the night.

Suspended in a moving night
The face in the reflected train
Looks at first sight as self-assured
As your own face — But look again:

Windows between you and the world
Keep out the cold, keep out the fright;
Then why does your reflection seem
So lonely in the moving night.

LOUIS MACNEICE

From a Flat City

Sometimes from the top deck of a bus
or the apogee of the Big Wheel at a fairground
you suddenly see them, like a pencil-smudge
or a brush-stroke of blue ink over the stacked
concrete blocks of the Hulme estate and the meat-pink
brick of the cavernous textile-mills at Reddish,
and say, 'the hills!' as if they were paying a rare,
auspicious visit. Not the prisoner's square
of sky is what we crave: we've that already,
a luminous, entrancing sky that hangs
its clouds above us, delicate and massive,
like a woman leaning over a sleepy lover.
It's earth we long for – earth heaped up like clouds,
drifted like smoke, smeared like approaching rain,
combed into escarpments or piled with forest.
Our imagination dwells in hills, but the plain
and the industrial haze deny them: it's
an achievement if you can make out Beeston Hill
from the eighteenth floor of the University Maths Tower.
Yet one morning, from my daughter's bedroom window,
between the shoulders of two redtiled roofs
I caught sight of a neat triangular peak
distinct from the clouds, apparently grassgrown, the sunlight
just dusting one edge. I had half a mind
(but that such accuracy is beyond me)
to take a compass-bearing, find a map,
identify the hill and one clear day
climb it with binoculars to sift
that window like a grain of glittering quartz
out of the city blur, and maybe see her
run to the glass and stare unseeing back
towards the hills she doesn't know are there.

Intersection

We think it's a dream or someone else's memory
until again it intersects, as it did that night,
full moon in the midcloud of damp November –
the trees like standing webs black against blue
mist, droplets tangible in the air,
and at a break in the hedge a furred gate,
split grain barred with darkness. Beyond it
fields swelling downwards, a fallow like brown bread,
chalked grassland, spinneys of slate, the glaze and powder
of tones mixed and rinsed on the moon's palette.
And as I had almost expected, there was a stile
at the field-corner, not alone but with a signpost
over it: nothing legible in that wooden gesture
except the difference of the path and an hour
still early by the moon's progress. Standing still
long enough to acknowledge the invitation
with an answering silence seemed necessary; and though
that path wasn't taken, pursuing the road again
was a knowledge that more than places are visited
in time, that what we know on the edge of sleep
is a part of our direction; the unique echo
of our footfalls is right when, as we think, it tells us
we're perhaps neither accidental nor alone.

Clun Castle

How did it happen that at sunset I was there
climbing the mound as if I had woken into a dream
and it was important to push my way up the tussocky grass
towards a skyline seen only as a dark edge
rimming the fractured halves of the castle keep? Bats
reeled from the weedhung faces of the stone
to flip and orbit against the peacock-blue
depth of the air, then weld themselves back
in a trice to the crannies and outcrops of rubble.
The dressed stone of the West wall so kept the sun's light
that to the mind's ear it sang as it cooled
over the loop of river, lost in its glassy shadows and brood
of mistgathering trees, to the easy Welsh hills
fired and hummocked like clouds into the scarlet lake of sky.
And how could it be that almost from my feet
the hillside fell away, and there on the valley floor –
small enough to cover with the palm of a hand –
was a newly-reaped field, where someone had left
a few bales to lie, and in the midst a cart
with the tailboard down, half-loaded, as if
that task suspended by twilight were the most
ordinary labour in the world, as if
some equation were not poised there still between
promise and accomplishment, between an urge to follow
the sun's attenuation to its last green transparency
and a need to turn down again to the village,
between the gathering black of orchard and housetop
and the growing white molten bar of the moon?

Jets

Not even the sky is free of our graffiti:
air-currents all day long smudge and emboss
flock trails scrawled by planes over the blue
latitudes of summer. Fine crystals of ice
drawn by the billion through that high cloud-chamber
in the wake of our irritant particles of business,
haste, anxiety, longing to be elsewhere,
they leave the sky's intangible islands and cities
barred or netted with oblique lines. Beautiful
when a sinking sun touches them off, or a breeze
frets them to solvent lace, still they inscribe
our failure to leave anything unmarked, our helpless
filling-up of our own space, as we thicken the mind
with noise, with chatter, with a scratch-polish of dullness.
Or so the mind reflects, pondering its mirror
nature: and yet those fine-scarfed skeins express
tranquillity too and something vulnerable,
ephemeral, and though entirely our own, no less
assumed by nature than the pattern of Dorset fields
or the New Grange rock-incisions. Restlessness
is what we're made of, as much as breath or water:
you can read it there as another jet goes over
and the dwindling chord of its engine-music spreads
to a rolling monotone with a hint of thunder,
drawing a white thread into a haystack of clouds.

Kaleidoscope
after Verlaine

You will wake in a street at the heart of a town in a dream,
And it will be as if you had already lived:
A moment at once very vague and completely clear,
A dazzling sun that heaves itself out of the fog.

And Oh that cry on the sea, that voice in the woods...
It will be as if you had never understood anything,
A slow coming-to after countless reincarnations,
Each thing seeming more itself than ever before;

And in that street, at the heart of that magical village
Where the barrel-organs will grind out jigs in the evenings,
Where each café will have a cat asleep on the counter,
Where marching bands will cross the street playing music –

Each thing will be so fraught with meaning that you will expect
To die, the lovely tears will stream down your cheeks,
Sobs of laughter amidst the racket of wheels,
And you will call out to sweet death to come now...

The old words evocative as a bouquet of dried flowers!
The jagged music of dance-halls will wander across,
And widows with copper trinkets on their foreheads,
Peasant-women shoving their way through the crowd

Of idlers who joke at street-corners with hideous rogues
And old men without eyebrows, floury with scurf,
While two blocks away the urine-scented gutters
Are loud with the fireworks of some public festival.

It will all be exactly as if you dreamed, and awoke,
And fell asleep again and still dreamed on
Of the same fairytale, the same spangle of colours,
The watered-silk hum of a bee's flight through long summer grass.

The Nightingale
after Verlaine

Like scared birds breaking cover, crying shrilly,
All my memories hurl themselves against me,
Dive in among the yellowed foliage
Of my heart, an alder-trunk bent to its image
Poised on the dark blue surface-sheen of Regret,
Which flows nearby, a melancholy streamlet;
Dive in – and then, soothed by the damp, fresh breeze,
Their hideous uproar settles by degrees
Until, after a moment, all is silent
Except a single voice praising the Absent,
The voice (drenched with such vibrant sweetness) of
The nightingale, who was my own first love
And still sings as she did on the first day;
And while the moon's sad splendour lifts away,
Pallid and solemn, from the earth, its light
Flooding the melancholy summer's night
Heavy with silence and obscurity,
Still soothes with her crystalline lullaby,
Where wind-fraught cirrhus flowers on azure skies,
The tree that trembles and the bird that cries.

Echoes
For S.A.

Each evening, once the children were in bed,
I'd climb the garden wall and scramble off
its damp, bouldery top into hogweed and nettles
round the end of the building; then among moths and headstones
to the porch, where I could ease the latch up, gently
swing the door open and hang back from the threshold
to watch a blue-grey slice of window ahead
for the scrap of black that suddenly flicked across,
brief as a trick of the fading light, but again
and again, becoming real though no less strange
with repetition. Stepping into the nave,
I would hear a small continuous rumpling noise
like someone shaking and shaking a soft leather glove
that refused to come right side out, until the waft
of air hit my cheek as a pipistrelle completed
its lap and circled my head before diving away
down the length of the church. I'd strain my ears for something
beyond that dull flutter: a chirp, an echo, some key-
signature to the labyrinth of harmonics
the bat must be threading, the sibilant cat's-cradle
of tremors pitched from the hammerbeam roof, the layered
darkness marbled with intersecting coils
of notes fanned from its diapason of squawks
by diffraction around the sandstone pillars, the floor
a stone pool whose reflective surface glinted
fugitive barks and cadenzas, except where I
was planted, a plume of muffling vapours, lit
by the flare of a curious moth. I could distinguish
nothing, though as I walked to the door my shoe-soles
released, I suppose, scuffed cymbal-crashes that burst
like surf up the walls, their last resonance dissolving
into the throat of the bell as I latched the door
with its figured bass of iron.
                                        Later that summer
we rented another house six miles away
down the coast, near a field where a noctule hunted at sunset,
ranging slowly across the sky – a small
black bird, it seemed, until it swooped and the frantic

flutter of wings came clear, a labour of flying
quite different from the hurtling glide of the swifts
with which sometimes it hunted. Taking a path
where corn-marigold and scabious straggled on
at the dusty margins of the wind-combed grasscrop,
I was almost afraid, the first time, of two people
inhumanly still, and watching me from the slope
at the western end of the field. I stared them out
and strode on over the clods as if I knew
where I was going and who owned the place
until I could see their rubber-glove hands, their faces
of swathed blue polythene sack. Standing beside them
to watch the bat sweep overhead, across
rags and strips of apricot cloud, I could hear,
all at once, the *pew, pep-pew* of its cry, a metallic
pizzicato twitched from the sky, and sensed
how the field with its drifts and spirals of air, its crop
of faintly seething insects, might be mapped
in a trawl of twilight echoes. Up at the gate
near the cliff-edge I turned and waved back at the house –
though I couldn't tell if you saw, the windows were merely
tiles of flame set into the grey slate wall –
a ritual I repeated each evening we stayed there.
The bat persisted too, even after the field
had been scalped and baled for silage, and the scarecrows
leant in a distant corner, their heads together
as if comparing notes, somehow attuned
to subtleties I had already missed.

The Beck

It was the boiling of white water drew me first:
a chant and turmoil in spate
under a scarlet-clustered rowan
that fluttered unceasingly, as if outside time,
vibrant and motionless at once in the beating of spray;
and the water foaming as if new-uttered that moment
from the earth's interior. Palms on the lichened rocks
(which were alive too with the presence of water)
I lowered myself into the cleft and drank
from cupped hands with a sudden
fierce thirst, as if I had never drunk
water before. And never such stunningly cold,
piercingly pure, flavourless and, it seemed,
evanescent water had I swallowed
until that instant. I would think, I promised,
of that water reciting itself without pause
here, wherever I might be, however preoccupied,
tired or bored, I would remember this,
rock, rowan and water.
                            But in my dream,
months later, it was a silent thread falling
from a mountainside above me, only breaking
to sound and spray when it splashed on the page of a book
which lay drenched and open under its downpour;
my task to climb the tussocked grass and rock
to reach it. I woke, lifting the unblemished pages,
and knew it was time to leave, to begin the next
ascent, unprepared as always, except for the taste
in my mouth of that water about which nothing can be said.

III

Grandfather's Books

The Fairy Books, of course:
   in one room or another
though mostly unremarked
   they have always been there.

With the gloom and glow
   of their handled reds and greens,
gold stamping and dogroses
   gathered on their spines

and proud pale women
   poised in the hooped thickets
of honeysuckle and thornstems
   after Dulac and Ricketts

they are the edge of a world,
   fringes of a wood
deeper than one lifetime.
   I was born in that wood.

I was a changeling
   who knew Jacobs and Lang,
gnarled Grimm and wily Yeats,
   the King of the Cats

– and would be king myself
   for a while. Should it happen,
it would be because I carried
   from their hands a talisman.

Aeneas' golden bough
   and Irene's thread,
they gleam darkly
   out of the same twilight,

they persist into day
   and leave us no choice
but to perform the part
   their windings rehearse.

Or no real choice.
   It has been like that with me,
the edge of the wood never
   very far away.

And when I die:
   shall I want to go
into that wood again?
   I don't know, I don't know.

The Whitethorn Tree

At the midpoint of winter
  My flowers unfold,
Starring the early dark under Orion
  With sparks of gold,
White petals stiff under the velvet frost
  In the dawn's cold.

Grown from no seed, I ripen
  Towards no fruit;
Cut from another of my own sparse kind
  I strike a root
In common earth, and wait for no successor
  To spring up at my foot.

You will wonder at me
  And as you go
If you should turn back momentarily
  You will not know
If those are fallen petals you can see
  Or the unmelted snow.

The Rosebush

'O little bird, what song do you sing,
    So full of music and of pain?
Little bird, come here to my window
    And sing your song again.'

O jeweller, jeweller, stop your work,
    Give me that gold watch and chain,
And I will perch outside your window
    And sing my song again:
        My mother killed me,
        My father ate me,
        My brother weeps and hangs his head;
        And here sing I from this rosebush,
        Stick, stock, stone dead.

'Little bird, little bird, what music is this
    Falls so sadly on my ear?
I must hear you sing it a second time
    Though it shakes my heart with fear.'

O cobbler, put down your awl and thread,
    Stop cobbling sole and shoe.
You must give me that pair of fine red boots
    Before I can sing for you:
        My mother killed me,
        My father ate me,
        My brother weeps and hangs his head;
        And here sing I from this rosebush,
        Stick, stock, stone dead.

'What is this song that echoes down
    Cool as a waterfall?
I would hunt the forests all my life through
    To hear that sweet bird's call.'

O mason, drop your hammer and chisel,
  Roll me that heavy millstone,
And I will sing you a colder song
  Than ever your heart has known:
    My mother killed me,
    My father ate me,
    My brother weeps and hangs his head;
    And here sing I from this rosebush,
    Stick, stock, stone dead.

'What is that sound like thunder that breaks
  About the roof and wall?
Go out and look if a storm is rising,
  For I fear the house will fall.'

O Father dear, you meant no harm,
  Nor knew what was in the dish;
You wanted a gold watch and chain
  And I have brought your wish.

And little brother who weep for me,
  Your love was always true:
You dreamed of a pair of fine red boots
  And I have brought them you.

But come out into the garden, Mother,
  Where you used to comb my hair;
But do not look for your brush and comb,
  You will not find them there.

But you will find an axe and billet
  Where you cut off my head,
For I rattle at your eaves with a millstone, Mother,
  And now it shall strike you dead.
    My mother killed me,
    My father ate me,
    My brother weeps and hangs his head;
    And here sing I from the housetop,
    Stick, stock, stone dead.

A First Dream

A round tower room:
I had climbed stone steps
And there was a little man,
Some gnome or dwarf perhaps.
He showed me a pair of shoes,
And this was all he said:
'They're very old, you know.'
And O I was seized
With a horror unspeakable.

'*Very old...old...*' – the word
Echoed through my struggle
To breathe, to wake.
And even now as I write
I am shocked to feel my hair prickle,
My skin crawling with terror
At the mere distant rumour,
The tremor of that ordeal.

And why should this be?
From that night to this
Never have I known
But can only guess
That the reason, the reason
Lay at the root of me.

I was a small child.
Did I fear old things, old people?
Or fear what would become of me
When I should grow old myself?
No, it was time, I guess,
Time itself that I feared,
And the death I had died already
That was still too close, too close,
That lay under that staircase,
That gaped like a well for me.

'And what became of the shoes?
And did you put them on?'

– Ah, though I fled, I fled,
It may be that I did,
It may be I put them on.

Recumbent Buddha at Polonnaruwa

A grain like marbling or like watered silk
flows without movement through the sleeping face:
rock-ripples tinged with rose and ash and milk,
known tastes of being, calmed, finding their place.

It is as though the rock itself had slept
to dream this shape, the eyelid's curve, the lip
smoother than any natural form except
maybe the moon's rim or a water-drop;

or as if we had sought a word to speak
out of our nature, suffering, changeable,
empty, and found at last simply this cheek
relaxing on clasped hands, and this half-smile

that flowers from more than a child's unblemished seeing
or a god's detachment. Massive, lightly creased,
the carved silk pillows a wholly human being
whose last breath has perhaps this moment ceased.

Notes

Patchwork   The sequence uses fifteen different rhyme-schemes. VII is an 'unrhymable' sonnet, written to the fourteen words listed in Swann and Sidgwick's *The Making of English Verse* as having no rhymes in English. XII is 'Meredithian'.

Meudon   Rilke worked as Rodin's secretary, living at his house and studio at Meudon near Paris during 1905-6. The poem draws loosely on accounts of this period, and incorporates some images from *The Notebook of Malte Laurids Brigge* and from E.M. Butler's *Rainer Maria Rilke* (1941).